ONE RANT A DAY

A cathartic daily journal

Hardie Grant

QUADRILLE

RANT OR *OR*

RAGE

Trumpet SHOUT

ADMONISH

BERA

PONTIFICATE

BELLOW YE

BLUSTER

SPOUT Hold fo

DELIVER A

ROAR

TE

HARANGUE

Declaim

LL

Sound off

LAMBAST

Fulminate

RANT

th

EXCORIATE

AND

TIRADE

RAVE

VERB
Speak or shout at length in an angry, impassioned way

NOUN
A spell of ranting; a tirade

THE HEART SPEEDS, THE PALMS SWEAT, THE MOUTH DRIES, AND THE SKIN PRICKLES. AND HERE IT COMES:

THE RANT

Indulging in a volley of vociferous verbal verbiage requires all senses to be on red alert. Afterwards, the stress hormone cortisol decreases – the body has been purged, the rant has restored the equilibrium.

WHY DO WE RANT?

1 VIOLATION OF THE NATURAL ORDER

SUCH AS...

- Queue jumper – we are NOT standing in line for FUN
- Idiots who take 20 items to a checkout meant for ONLY "10 items or fewer"
- Parking hogs who take up TWO spaces

2 VIOLATION OF EXPECTATION

SUCH AS...

- "Cash only"
- No Wi-Fi
- Discovering the sticky tape has run out just as you're about to wrap the gifts

3 REPETITION OF INFURIATING BEHAVIOUR

SUCH AS...

- *"Will someone else PLEASE replace the toilet paper for once?"*
- The friend who is ALWAYS late
- *"Socks / wet towels / sports kit do NOT live on MY bedroom floor"*

4 OBSTRUCTIONS TO YOUR GOAL

SUCH AS...

- Following a slow driver
- *Dry Clean Only*
- Slamming train/bus doors

5 FEELING IMPOTENT

SUCH AS...

- *"But that's not what I said..."*
- *"No you don't understand..."*
- *"No, I can't remember my password"*

FRUSTI

1 **The feeling of being upset or annoyed as a result of being unable to change or achieve something.**

2 **The prevention of the progress, success, or fulfilment of something.**

OR...

3 **The wild scream that surges within when you realize there is no more coffee.**

4 **The success of others.**

RATION

"ANGER IS AN ACID THAT CAN DO MORE HARM TO THE VESSEL IN WHICH IT IS STORED THAN TO ANYTHING ON WHICH IT IS POURED."*

MARK TWAIN

*(In other words – that rant you want to shout to the rooftops is better out than in.)

Moaning: *the glorious vocal release of pleasure.* (And no, not in the bedroom. This definition surely refers to having a good old rant.)

THE ACTOR PETER SELLERS KEPT A "SHIT LIST"

Updated daily, Sellers's list included those in his professional and personal life whom he found to be irritating, obstructive or just downright rude.

TRY IT – it's the most extraordinary fun.

A PROBLEM SHARED IS A PROBLEM HALVED.*

*Well it's not really though, is it?
You're still the one removing the
apple cores from under the bed...
finishing the report on time...on the
phone, 49th in line for customer services.

TOP PLACES TO RANT AND RAVE:

1 In this journal

2 With your friends swimming in a bucket of gin

3 Into your pillow, alone with your tears

4 In the nuzzle of your favourite pet

5 At the hairdressers over a copy of a trashy magazine

6 In wide open spaces

7 In a mosh pit where no one can hear you scream

BAD PLACES TO RANT AND RAVE:

1 On social media (yes, everyone else does it, but you're better than that)

2 At airport security

3 Across your dating profile

4 During a job interview

5 On a budget airline when they charge for water

6 Around the dinner table (unless you're Italian)

7 At your anniversary party

"I'M NOT INSULTING YOU, I'M DESCRIBING YOU"

IS THERE ANYTHING MORE ANNOYING THAN ANNOYING PEOPLE?

✓

The woman at the gym who hogs the hair-drying space with all her products ☐

The sociopath who thought sleeveless cardigans were a good idea ☐

Any driver who tailgates you relentlessly ☐

The YouTube influencer ☐

The neighbour who complains about *everything* ☐

The referee who always makes the wrong call ☐

People who recommend podcasts ☐

Anyone who, when asked if they're well, responds with *"Well actually I've had a bit of a bad spell recently"* and proceeds to go *on and on and on* about it ☐

The delivery driver who left your parcel in the drain ☐

That maniac receptionist at the clinic who seems delighted when you report your latest symptom ☐

The delivery guy who left a "sorry we missed you" note when YOU WERE IN! ☐

The dreary soul who made us all believe *mushroom* and *light turd* were tasteful colours with which to paint our houses ☐

Anyone who drops litter ☐

Other people's children ☐

Your own children ☐

Cyclists ☐

People who moan about cyclists ☐

Your parents ☐

Your in-laws ☐

Your siblings ☐

Your friends ☐

Yours friends' partners ☐

Your partner ☐

Your partner's friends ☐

Your partner's friends' girlfriends ☐

You ☐

"HE IS SIMPLY A HOLE IN THE AIR"

GEORGE ORWELL
The Lion and the Unicorn

"IF I WAS
IGNO
AS YOU I
LET

AS

RANT

WOULDN'T

ON"

MARK TWAIN
*The Adventures
of Huckleberry Finn*

Which acts of flagrant stupidity, by your colleagues or family members, have left you howling at the moon at their blatant idiocy?

_____

_____

_____

_____

_____

_____

_____

_____

_____

_____

_____

_____

_____

OF ALL THE PEOPLE IN THE WORLD WHO IRRITATE YOU THE MOST, ODDS ON, IT'S YOU.

Treat yourself as a separate entity and record exactly how annoying you are.

NOUN
The release or expression of
a strong emotion, energy etc.

VERB
Give free expression to
(a strong emotion)

EXAMPLE
*"Please excuse me for a
moment while I vent about
green bananas..."*

WHAT IS MORE RANT INDUCING THAN...

1 **Waiting in line at the Post Office and seeing at least four officials behind the counter but ONLY ONE CHECKOUT OPEN**

2 **The _"This checkout is closing"_ sign being placed just as you arrive with a full shopping cart**

3 **NO delivery slots left for the online order**

"Anybody can become angry, that is easy; but to be angry with the right person and to the right degree and at the right time and for the right purpose, and in the right way – that is not within everybody's power and is not easy."

ARISTOTLE

Ranting is one of the most effective forms of communication. It expresses more information more rapidly than almost any other style of emotion.

IF I HAVE TO...

Deal with a self-service checkout that doesn't work...

Pick up an automated phone call...

Remember yet another password...

ONE MORE TIME, I WILL…

...leave the shop empty-handed and eat stale bread from the back of the cupboard just to prove a point.

...swap my smartphone for a brick.

..."sign in as guest" and then not buy anything just to prove another very important point.

"WHEN ANGRY, COUNT TO FOUR...

WHEN VERY ANGRY, SWEAR"

MARK TWAIN

HAVEN'T GOT ENOUGH TIME TO GET CROSS WITH FULLY-FLEDGED WORDS?

Try these handy acronyms instead.

FFS ➝ **For fuck's sake**

AIBU ➝ **Am I being unreasonable**

HTH ➝ **Hope this helps (*Oh get lost with your passive-aggressive-I-know-best rubbish*)**

JFGI ➝ **Just fucking Google it**

MYOB ➝ **Mind your own business**

NBC ➝ **Nobody cares**

IDC ➝ **I don't care**

Rant	➡	English
Përçartje	➡	Albanian
Bulderen	➡	Dutch
Paasaus	➡	Finnish
Henceg	➡	Hungarian
Vociferar	➡	Portuguese
Declama	➡	Romanian
Despotricar	➡	Spanish

The word *rant* emerged c.1600 meaning, "To be jovial and boisterous" or "To talk bombastically". *Rant* derives from the Dutch word *randten*.

Fuchsteufelswild (adj)

UNTRANSLATABLE GERMAN WORD, LOOSELY MEANING:

Pure animal rage – fox-devil wild

"A RANT A DAY KEEPS THE ANGER AWAY"

KVETCH

NOUN
A person who complains
a great deal

VERB
Complain persistently

Document the people whose persistent moaning and negative attitude really rile you. Honestly, if only they would stop complaining.

_____

_____

_____

_____

_____

_____

_____

_____

_____

_____

_____

_____

_____

_____

_____

_____

BEST RANT BY SHAKESPEARE

"A knave; a rascal; an eater of broken meats; a base, proud, shallow, beggarly three-suited, hundred-pound, filthy, worsted-stocking knave; a lily-livered, action-taking whoreson, glass-gazing, superserviceable, finical rogue; one-trunk-inheriting slave; one that wouldst be a bawd, in way of good service, and art nothing but the composition of a knave, beggar, coward, pander, and the son and heir of a mongrel bitch; one whom I will beat into clamorous whining, if thou deniest the least syllable of thy addition."

Spat out by Kent about Oswald, in Shakespeare's King Lear

If your own common decency, societal norms and the threat of prison were absent, how exactly would you rant, in your own perfect ranting paradise?

→ Drive a digger around town crushing all non-disabled cars in *Disabled Only* spaces?

→ Summon all the head designers, sit them down and don't let them leave until they've created sexy underwear that doesn't get stuck up your bum.

→ Tattoo social media trolls with their own awful words?

MEH PREGGERS

Behaviours SICK
(it's BEHAVIOUR)

VEGGIES

DD DRY

BRAINSTORM

LITERALLY Minion

YOURSELF (IT'S YO

MONETIZE
Toilet HUBBY
MYSELF (YOU MEAN I)
METHINKS
THINKPIECE DB
JANUARY
ANYTHING WITH A #
AMAZEBALLS SYNERGY
BANTZ
- NOT YOURSELF)

HAVE SMARTPHONES REALLY ADDED TO THE WELL OF HUMAN HAPPINESS?

"Just put it on silent"

People using phones when being served in a shop

"And turn the vibration off"

Photographing food

"Who still makes keypad noises?"

Lunatics who step into the road while looking at their phones

"No, I haven't just been involved in an accident"

ALL work emails AFTER work

"I'm just checking something"

Charging the phone without turning the socket on

"Where's my phone?"

No "likes" to any social media posts

"Why haven't they responded? I posted it one minute ago?"

Too many "likes" – it's getting weird now

SOCIAL MEDIA IRRITANTS

THE SELFIE DIVA

Enough already! One bikini shot is enough – it's winter

THE CONSTANT MEMER

They're just not funny

BABY-MAD PARENTS

Great that you're proud but yawn...
so bored...I can't finish this senten...

FAMILY FOLLOWERS

This update is *not* meant to be seen by you,
Dad. It's only a facial tattoo, don't judge

THE OVER-SHARER

Sorry you cut yourself shaving this morning
but there's no need to show the blood in the
shower tray...or the skin left in the razor...or the
stain on the carpet...or how your ankle stuck to
your tights...or the plaster you finally found...and
how it fell off on the station platform...and how
a fit man asked if you're ok...Just get your legs
waxed next time...And *don't* tell me about it.

NOISES THAT DRIVE YOU WILD

- → *Anything* in the Quiet Carriage
- → Rustling at the cinema
- → Wet coughs when you know phlegm is involved
- → The ostentatious laugh
- → Chewing

"IN MY MANY YEARS
I HAVE COME TO A
CONCLUSION THAT
ONE USELESS MAN
IS A SHAME, TWO IS
A LAW FIRM, AND
THREE OR MORE
IS A CONGRESS."

JOHN ADAMS
Founding Father and American President

Incompetence, idleness and downright idiocy in the workplace inspire ranters everywhere to bemoan their feckless colleagues. What most vexes you at work?

- [ ] Lateness

- [ ] Disorganization

- [ ] Micromanagement

- [ ] Endless sick days

- [ ] Gossiping

- [ ] Officiousness

- [ ] Favouritism

A survey by Samsung in 2016 revealed that 92% of workers complained about slow Internet and computers crashing.

Distractions from colleagues caused fellow workers to lose 22 minutes a day on average.

THE
DARKEST
OF DARK
RANTS

If only you weren't such a good
person and instead fessed up to
the things that you, in your darkest
moments, would love to have a
good rant about. Just whisper
them, no one will hear...

→ **People who talk about
their pets as if they were
children**

→ **Creepy male feminists**

→ **Anyone who talks about
their "journey"**

THE MOST ANNOYING PERSON IN THE WORLD?

ANYONE WHO "REPLIES ALL"

THE NON-RETURNER OF BORROWED ITEMS

THE SOCIAL SMOKER / VAPER (IN OTHER WORDS – THIEF)

WORST HABITS IN THE WORLD?

RETURNING EMPTY CONTAINERS TO THE FRIDGE

SNIFFING

HUMBLEBRAGGING

LEG JOGGLING

BEING VAGUE

ANNOYING PHRASES...

"YOU'RE DAMNED IF YOU DO,
DAMNED IF YOU DON'T."

"WE ARE WHERE WE ARE."

"IT IS WHAT IT IS."

"WHAT WILL BE WILL BE."

Ever fantasized about writing
an anonymous note and
leaving it on the desk of
your boss / most annoying
colleague / utterly useless
co-worker to discover what
they're really like?

Write away in the safety
of your journal...

" *Dear* [insert useless colleague's name here],

please stop chewing your sandwiches
so loudly right near my ear. If I want
to sit next to a cow, I'll move my desk
to a field. **"**

I TOLD YOU SO

Which events / scenarios / disasters have panned out exactly as you predicted. How bad were they?

WHO WILL YOU NEVER ACCEPT?

Which monsters will you never be able to accommodate in this free, open and inclusive world in which we are all supposed to live?

	✓
The woman who puts on a full face of makeup on public transport?	☐
The adolescent with the unpopped zit?	☐
The sententious man who speaks with his eyes closed?	☐
The child who sits with their mouth open?	☐
Anyone with loud headphones?	☐
People who mouth kiss their pets?	☐
Anyone who uses their children / pets on their social media profile picture?	☐
Backpacks with tourists attached?	☐
Parents with baby buggies in shops?	☐
All mouthbreathers?	☐

A rant need not necessarily have necessarily have a result. It does not need to force an apology or create a change. Rather, think of a rant as a high-octane, adrenaline-fuelled catharsis.

"I NEVER SAW ANYBODY TAKE SO LONG TO DRESS, AND WITH SUCH LITTLE RESULT"

OSCAR WILDE
The Importance of Being Earnest

From Instagram influencers to TV presenters and Hollywood princesses, there is nothing more annoying than celebrities inflicting their terrible fashion choices on the innocent public. Which celebrities have the worst...

Hair

Shoes

Smile

Clothes

Voice

Makeup

Choice in partners

BORING

Adjective

DEFINITION
Not interesting; tedious

SYNONYMS
Dreary
Dull
Monotonous
Tedious
Tiresome

NAME THE TASKS THAT SET YOU YAWNING

NAME THE PEOPLE THAT SET YOU SNORING

RATE OUT OF 10 HOW ANNOYING YOU FIND...

Pop-up ads

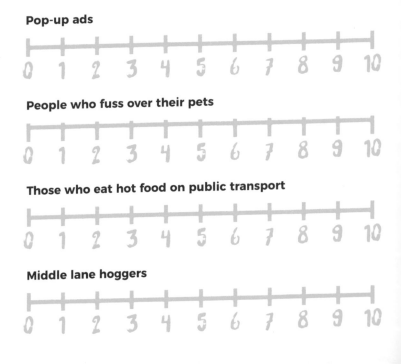

People who fuss over their pets

Those who eat hot food on public transport

Middle lane hoggers

People walking too slowly in front of you

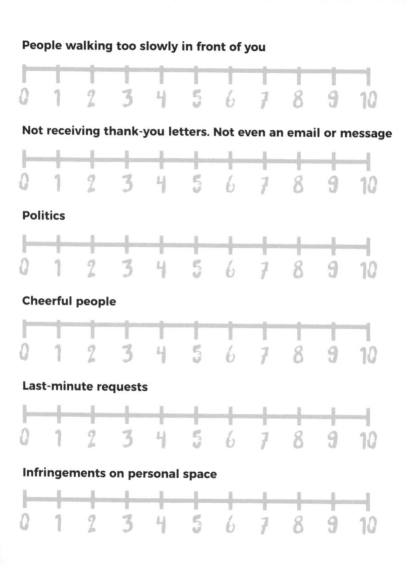

0 1 2 3 4 5 6 7 8 9 10

Not receiving thank-you letters. Not even an email or message

0 1 2 3 4 5 6 7 8 9 10

Politics

0 1 2 3 4 5 6 7 8 9 10

Cheerful people

0 1 2 3 4 5 6 7 8 9 10

Last-minute requests

0 1 2 3 4 5 6 7 8 9 10

Infringements on personal space

0 1 2 3 4 5 6 7 8 9 10

L'esprit de l'escalier

ROUGH TRANSLATION FROM FRENCH
(THERE IS NO EXACT ENGLISH EQUIVALENT):

The predicament of thinking up the perfect reply too late

IF ONLY I HAD SAID *THAT*...

(INSTEAD OF BLUSHING AND WALKING OFF WITHOUT RANTING MY COMPLAINT.)

ANGRY MUSIC FOR WHEN YOU NEED TO RANT (LOUDLY)

"I HATE EVERYTHING ABOUT YOU"

THREE DAYS GRACE
(Self-explanatory)

"CARMINA BURANA"

CARL ORFF
(It's all about the wheel of fortune – the piece gets really loud and cross when the wheel swings down to the depths of humanity)

"BREAK STUFF"

LIMP BIZKIT
(Let them break stuff, so you don't have to)

"SYMPHONY NUMBER 4 IN F MINOR"

RALPH VAUGHAN WILLIAMS
(Usually a pastoral composer, he got really cross with the rise of totalitarianism in 1930s Europe)

"FIRESTARTER"

PRODIGY
(Just shout your head off with them)

PURPOSEFUL RANTING

Sure, letting rip, having a rant, or even moaning under your breath, are great ways of alleviating red-hot-in-the-moment fury. However, what about a good purposeful rant, what about all those problems that have been niggling you for years? Put ranting to good use by addressing the issues you've always meant to.

How about...

➤ **Writing to your local representative about potholes / litter / knife crime**

➤ **Convening a meeting with your boss and HR about securing that pay rise**

SMALL RANTS

Today I shall have a small rant about the
few small things that get on my nerves…

- Crumbs
- Zits
- Hangovers

BiG RANTS

Today I shall have a big rant about the big things that are a complete nightmare

- Racism
- Climate change
- Hangovers

BEST
CELEBRITY
RANTS

When Serena Williams lost the US Open Championship

"I have never cheated in my life...
You owe me an apology...This is
not fair...You are a thief..."

**British journalist John Sweeney turning tomato red
and bellowing at a Scientologist**

"Now listen to me...
you were not there..."

**John McEnroe slamming down his
tennis racket and shouting**

"You cannot be serious"

at Wimbledon

**Prince Charles muttering under his breath about
the BBC's royal correspondent Nicholas Witchell**

"I hate that man.
He's so awful, he really is."

BRILLIANT BENEFITS

BENEFITS

OF RANTING

1 RESTORE JUSTICE

So, that person who tried to slip in front of you in the line, has been fairly sent to the back, everyone else is with you, and the correct social order has been restored. 1-0 to you and your rant.

2 RESTORE RELATIONSHIPS

Frankly, there was only so much more you could take. Thank goodness you've finally broached the subject of his nose picking. You can now enjoy the corporate away day with a quiet mind.

3 RESTORE POWER (YOUR OWN)

"Enough already – I'm in charge here!" So said those aggrieved folk at the 18th century Boston Tea Party. Get cross about an unfair tax, boot out the oppressive overlords and before you know it America is a free and independent nation.
Ranting American Freedom Fighters 1–0 British Empire.

"THE SUPREME TASK
IS TO ORGANIZE
AND UNITE PEOPLE
SO THAT THEIR
ANGER BECOMES
A TRANSFORMING
FORCE"

MARTIN LUTHER KING JR
Civil Rights Leader

MUTUAL RANTING FUN

Best people to rant with	Ranting subject	Equipment
Partners	Rent, mortgage, house, apartment, friends, children, jobs, bills, the world at large	Dinner and wine
School parents	Rubbish teachers, other people's children, homework, lack of homework	Tea and coffee at the school bake sale
Colleagues	Bosses, other colleagues, the workload, the culture, the salary	Watercooler
Best friends	Everything	Phones, wine, more wine, gin, cocktails, babysitter, Facebook, Instagram, Pinterest

MY FAVOURITE PEOPLE TO RANT WITH ARE...

THE
DOS
AND
DON'TS
OF
RANTING

Do

EXPRESS YOURSELF CLEARLY

USE FACTS NOT JUST FEELINGS

BE FAIR

BE HONEST

BE BRAVE

Don't

COMPLETELY LOSE YOUR SHIT

JUST MUTTER UNDER YOUR
BREATH (NO-ONE LIKES THAT)

GET PHYSICAL

VERBAL ONSLAUGHT?

STIFF LETTER?

IRATE PHONE CALL?

According to the British Association of Anger Management, 65% of people are more likely to express anger over the phone compared to 26% in writing and 9% face to face.

PASSIVE AGGRESSIVE OR HOT-TEMPERED RANTER?

PASSIVE AGGRESSIVE

"I DIDN'T MEAN TO UPSET YOU."

"OH, I THOUGHT YOU UNDERSTOOD."

"SSSSSSHHHHHHHHHHHH"

HOT-TEMPERED

"@!!*#*!!"

"I WILL NOT KEEP CALM AND YOU CAN FUCK OFF."

"YOU'LL BE HEARING FROM MY SOLICITOR."

If you've had enough of ranting –
think about moving. The UN's 2018
World Happiness Report lists the
happiest countries in the world.

TOP 5 HAPPIEST COUNTRIES, 2018
1. Finland
2. Norway
3. Denmark
4. Iceland
5. Switzerland

**Initial ranting response to this
bit of sunny polling?**

I don't believe it for a minute.

What about the cold?

Huh – I bet they're seething inside.

Business Development Director Melanie Gray
Editor Céline Hughes
Author Joanna Gray
Designer Katherine Keeble
Production Director Vincent Smith
Production Controller Nikolaus Ginelli

Published in 2019 by Quadrille,
an imprint of Hardie Grant Publishing

Quadrille
52–54 Southwark Street
London SE1 1UN
quadrille.com

ISBN 978 1 78713 457 7

Printed in China